Ourselves

Peter Riley and Dr Brian Knapp

Curriculum Visions

Science@School

Teacher's Guide
There is a Teacher's Guide available
to accompany this book.

Dedicated Web Site
There is a wealth of supporting
material including videos and activities
available at the Professional Zone,
part of our dedicated web site:

www.CurriculumVisions.com

The Professional Zone
is a subscription zone.

A CVP Book.
First published in 2008

Copyright © 2008 Earthscape

Authors
*Peter Riley, BSc, C Biol, MI Biol, PGCE,
and Brian Knapp, BSc, PhD*

Senior Designer
Adele Humphries, BA, PGCE

Educational Consultant
*Jan Smith (former Deputy Head of Wellfield School,
Burnley, Lancashire)*

Editor
Gillian Gatehouse

Designed and produced by
EARTHSCAPE

Printed in China by
WKT Co., Ltd

**Curriculum Visions Science@School
Volume 1A Ourselves**
*A CIP record for this book is available
from the British Library.*
ISBN: 978 1 86214 253 4

Picture credits
All pictures are from the Earthscape and
ShutterStock collections.

*This product is manufactured from sustainable
managed forests. For every tree cut down at least one
more is planted.*

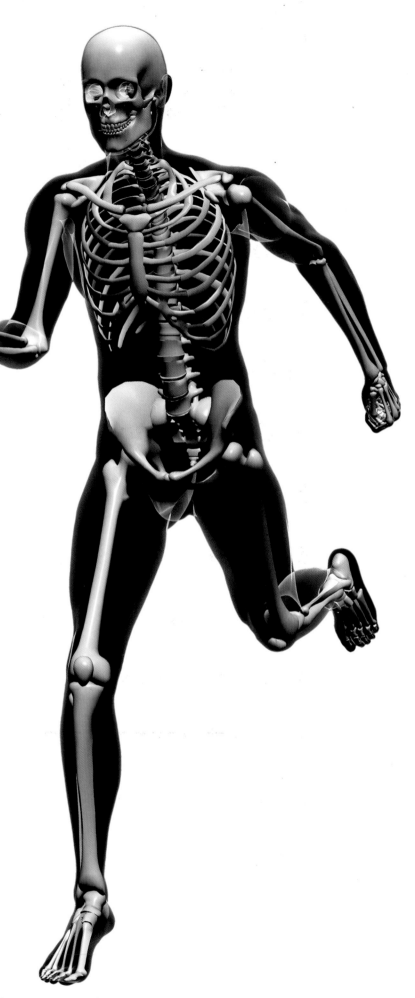

There are bones inside our bodies.

Contents

Page

Weblink: www.curriculumvisions.com

Your body

There are many parts to your body.

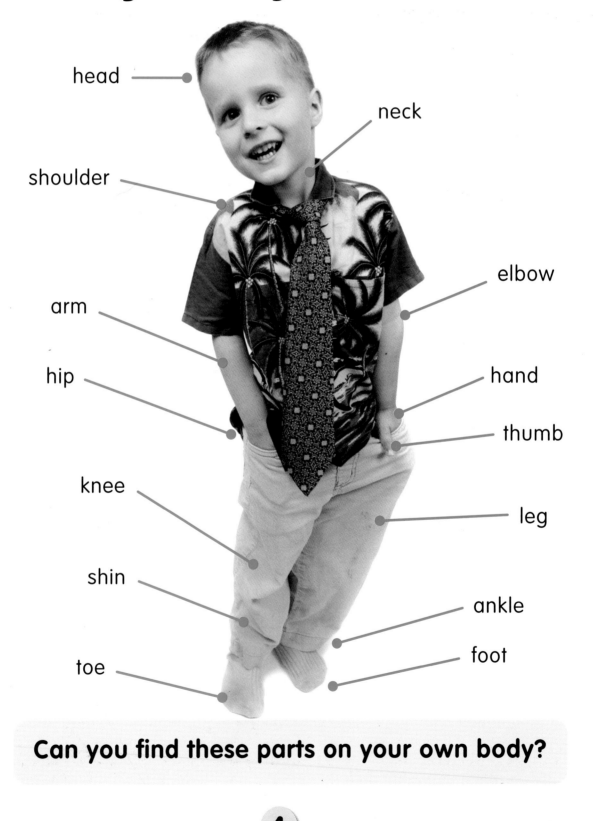

head

neck

shoulder

elbow

arm

hand

hip

thumb

knee

leg

shin

ankle

toe

foot

Can you find these parts on your own body?

Weblink: www.curriculumvisions.com

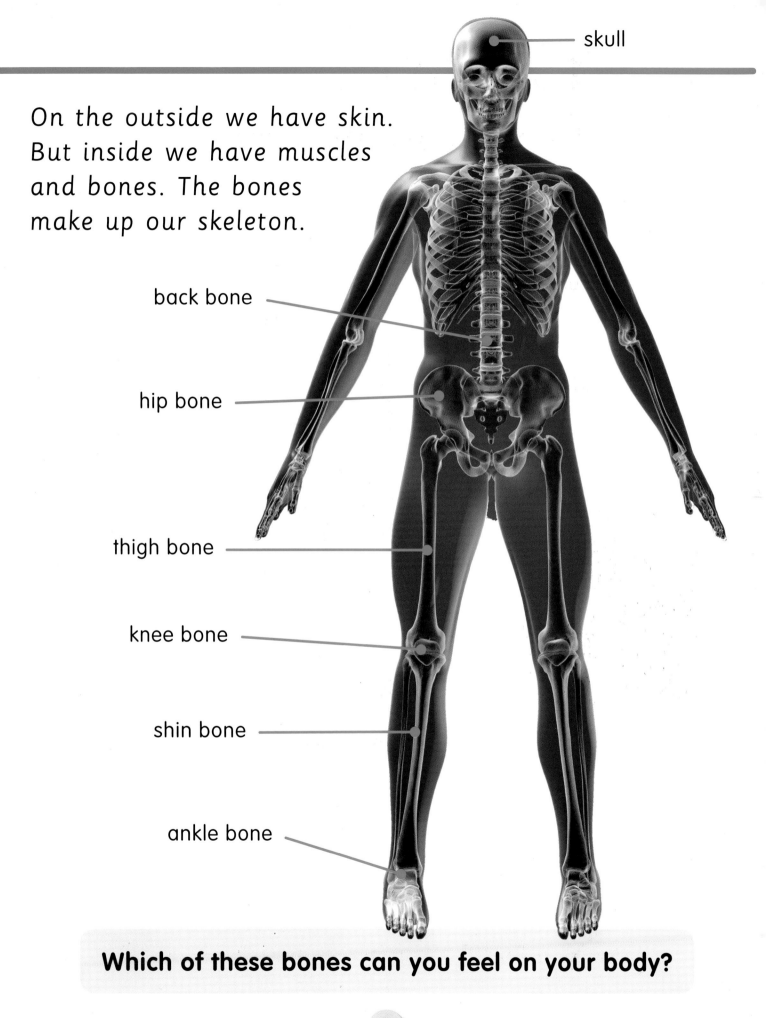

On the outside we have skin. But inside we have muscles and bones. The bones make up our skeleton.

skull

back bone

hip bone

thigh bone

knee bone

shin bone

ankle bone

Which of these bones can you feel on your body?

Weblink: www.curriculumvisions.com

Senses

We use senses to tell us about the world around us.

We use five ways to know about our world.

They are called our senses.

They are seeing, hearing, touching, tasting and smelling.

1. We see with our eyes.

2. We hear with our ears.

Weblink: www.curriculumvisions.com

3. We touch
with our hands.

4. We taste with our tongue.

5. We smell with our nose.

What can you see now?

What can you hear now?

Weblink: www.curriculumvisions.com

Growing up

We grow from babies to old people.

Babies grow up into children.

Children become grown-ups.

A baby.

Young children with their parents.

Grown-ups change, too.

Their hair may stop growing.

They may get wrinkles.

Their hair may go grey.

little hair

wrinkles

A middle-aged
grown-up.

grey hair

An old
grown-up.

How will you change as you grow up?

Weblink: www.curriculumvisions.com

Our food and drink

We need to eat and drink to keep us healthy.

Many animals eat just one kind of food.

But we are different.

We need many types of food to stay healthy.

A healthy dinner of chicken and vegetables.

chicken

vegetables

Milk and cookies.

A beefburger.

A good breakfast with lots to drink.

What is your favourite meal? Is it healthy?

Weblink: www.curriculumvisions.com

5 Animals

There are many kinds of animal.

We have lots of names for animals.

We call some of them fish.

We call some birds.

We call others insects.

Animals like ourselves are called mammals.

Goldfish

Tiger

12

Butterfly

Spider

Caterpillar

Frog

Ourselves

How many other animals can you think of?

Weblink: www.curriculumvisions.com

What animals do

Animals move about.

Animals eat, drink and breathe.

They move about.

They have babies, and they grow.

An elephant drinking.

A mouse eating cheese.

Camels walking in a desert.

Weblink: www.curriculumvisions.com

A baboon
carrying
its baby.

Mum and dad giraffe caring for their baby.

Do things that are not alive eat, drink and breathe?

Weblink: www.curriculumvisions.com

Baby animals

Baby animals grow up quickly.

Baby animals grow up fast.

They get bigger and bigger.

egg

A chick is a baby chicken.

A puppy is a baby dog.

Weblink: www.curriculumvisions.com

sheep

lamb

A lamb grows up to be a sheep.

A foal grows up
to be a horse.

horse

foal

What does a kitten grow up to be?

Weblink: www.curriculumvisions.com

Animals move

Animals move in many ways.

Some animals use their legs to move.

Birds use their wings.

Fish wiggle their bodies.

A horse gallops.

Weblink: www.curriculumvisions.com

A bird flies.

eagle

A cat prowls.

A fish swims.

How does a rabbit move?   **How does a snake move?**

Weblink: www.curriculumvisions.com

What animals eat

Animals mostly eat just one kind of food.

A chicken eats seeds.

Every animal needs its own special kind of food.

That is why cats, dogs and rabbits do not have the same food as us.

A squirrel eats nuts.

A dog eats meat and biscuits.

A snail eats leaves.

A deer eats grass.

What does a cat eat?

Words to learn

Breathe

Take in air then push it out.

Caterpillar

A young insect before it grows wings.

Gallop

The way a horse runs with all its feet leaving the ground at once.

Weblink: www.curriculumvisions.com

Muscles

Parts of the body that move bones and skin.

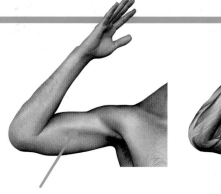

arm with skin   muscles under skin

Skeleton

The bones inside the body.

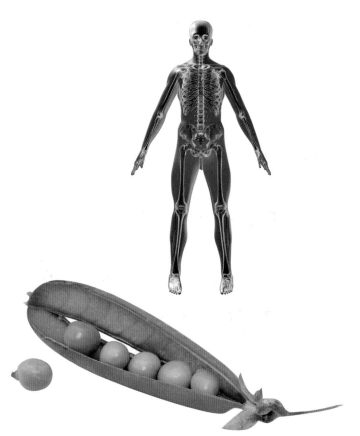

Vegetables

Food from the leaves, seeds and roots of plants. Cabbages, peas and carrots are vegetables.

Wrinkles

Lines in the skin of an old person.

Weblink: www.curriculumvisions.com

Index